Rosa Parks
Activist for Equality

by Grace Hansen

Abdo
HISTORY MAKER BIOGRAPHIES
Kids

abdopublishing.com

Published by Abdo Kids, a division of ABDO, PO Box 398166, Minneapolis, Minnesota 55439.

Copyright © 2016 by Abdo Consulting Group, Inc. International copyrights reserved in all countries. No part of this book may be reproduced in any form without written permission from the publisher.

Printed in the United States of America, North Mankato, Minnesota.

102015

012016

THIS BOOK CONTAINS
RECYCLED MATERIALS

Photo Credits: AP Images, Corbis, Getty Images, iStock, Library of Congress, Shutterstock

Production Contributors: Teddy Borth, Jennie Forsberg, Grace Hansen

Design Contributors: Laura Mitchell, Dorothy Toth

Library of Congress Control Number: 2015941770

Cataloging-in-Publication Data

Hansen, Grace.

 Rosa Parks: activist for equality / Grace Hansen.

   p. cm. -- (History maker biographies)

Includes index.

ISBN 978-1-68080-126-2

1. Parks, Rosa, 1913-2005--Juvenile literature. 2. African American women--Alabama--Montgomery--Juvenile literature. 3. Civil rights workers--Alabama--Montgomery--Biography--Juvenile literature. 1. Title.

323/092--dc23

[B]

2015941770

Table of Contents

Birth & Early Life 4

The Bus 10

Change 14

Death & Legacy 20

Timeline. 22

Glossary 23

Index 24

Abdo Kids Code. 24

Birth & Early Life

Rosa McCauley was born on February 4, 1913. She was born in Tuskegee, Alabama.

Alabama

Rosa and her family moved to Montgomery, Alabama. The city had **Jim Crow laws**. These laws separated blacks and whites.

OUR CHILDREN PLAY TOGETHER WHY CANT THEY LEARN TOGETHER
I CANT GO TO SCHOOL BECAUSE OF SEGREGATION.

At 19, Rosa married Raymond Parks. He was a barber. Rosa was a **seamstress**. But she wanted to do more. She joined the **NAACP** in 1943.

9

The Bus

On December 1, 1955, Rosa got on the bus. She sat in the section for blacks. The seats for whites were full. The driver told Rosa to move to make more room.

Rosa refused to move.

She was tired of the unfair

laws. She was put in jail.

13

Change

On December 5, Rosa went to trial. The **NAACP** planned a **boycott** on the same day. No black person would ride the buses until laws changed.

15

On November 13, 1956, the **Supreme Court** ruled. It said that **segregation** was unfair. The **boycott** ended on December 20.

17

Laws changed in Montgomery. But racism was still there. The Parkses moved to Detroit, Michigan. They were happy there.

Death & Legacy

Rosa died on October 24, 2005.

She proved that a small act

could make a big change.

21

Timeline

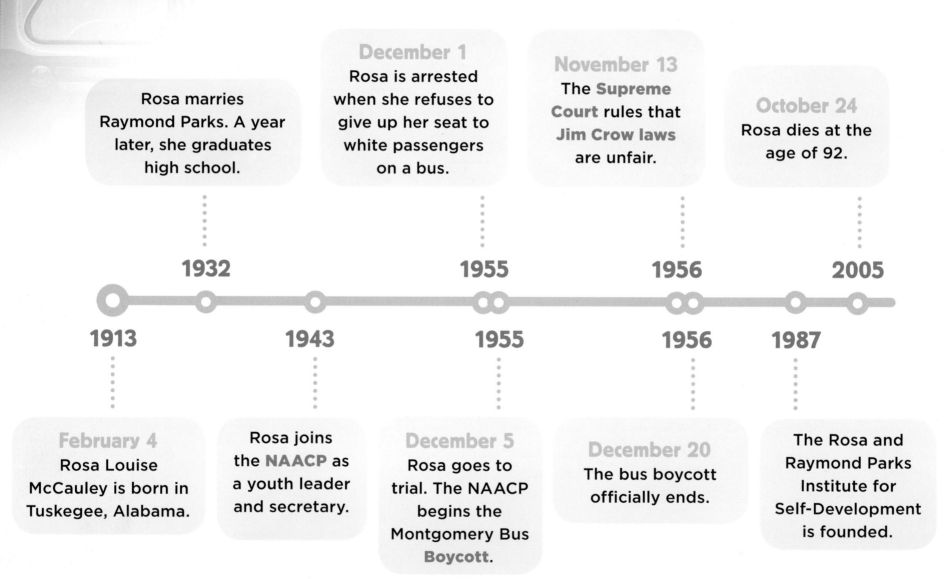

December 1
Rosa is arrested when she refuses to give up her seat to white passengers on a bus.

Rosa marries Raymond Parks. A year later, she graduates high school.

November 13
The **Supreme Court** rules that **Jim Crow laws** are unfair.

October 24
Rosa dies at the age of 92.

1932

1955

1956

2005

1913

1943

1955

1956

1987

February 4
Rosa Louise McCauley is born in Tuskegee, Alabama.

Rosa joins the **NAACP** as a youth leader and secretary.

December 5
Rosa goes to trial. The NAACP begins the Montgomery Bus **Boycott**.

December 20
The bus boycott officially ends.

The Rosa and Raymond Parks Institute for Self-Development is founded.

Glossary

boycott – an act of joining with others to ban a certain person, product, place, or organization.

Jim Crow laws – state and local laws that made racial segregation legal in the Southern United States.

NAACP – stands for the National Association for the Advancement of Colored People. The organization formed in 1909 to ensure equality of rights of all persons, and to end racism.

seamstress – a woman whose job is sewing.

segregation – the act of separating people based on gender, race, or something else. Jim Crow laws made this legal in the South.

Supreme Court – the highest court of a state or of the U.S.

23

Index

birth 4

bus 10

death 20

Detroit, Michigan 18

Jim Crow Laws 6, 10, 12

marriage 8

Montgomery, Alabama 6, 18

NAACP 8, 14

Supreme Court 16

Tuskegee, Alabama 4

abdokids.com

Use this code to log on to abdokids.com and access crafts, games, videos, and more!

Abdo Kids Code:
HRK1262